Shark with a

Written by Rachael Davis

Illustrated by Borghild Fallberg

Collins

Look! Can you see?
Might it be ...

... a bat in a hat?
Think of that!

A goat in a boat?

Look at that coat!

A bee yelling wee?

Not that I see!

A shark in a park?

Wow, it can bark!

A cow yelling pow?

Not right now!

But at night,
we all might ...